Hey, A**hole!

You Probably Need These, Too

Hey, A**hole!

Art to Color
for the Losers in Your Life

ST. MARTIN'S GRIFFIN
NEW YORK

ZENDOODLE COLORING PRESENTS HEY, A**HOLE!
Copyright © 2016 by St. Martin's Press. All rights reserved.
Printed in the United States of America. For information, address
St. Martin's Press, 175 Fifth Avenue, New York, N.Y. 10010.

www.stmartins.com

ISBN 978-1-250-12681-8 (trade paperback)

Our books may be purchased in bulk for promotional, educational,
or business use. Please contact your local bookseller or the
Macmillan Corporate and Premium Sales Department at
1-800-221-7945, extension 5442, or by e-mail
at MacmillanSpecialMarkets@macmillan.com.

First Edition: November 2016

10 9 8 7 6 5 4 3 2 1

With all
due respect,
you're an
asshole.

Let me count the ways . . .
you can go fuck yourself

We never talk
anymore.
I like that.

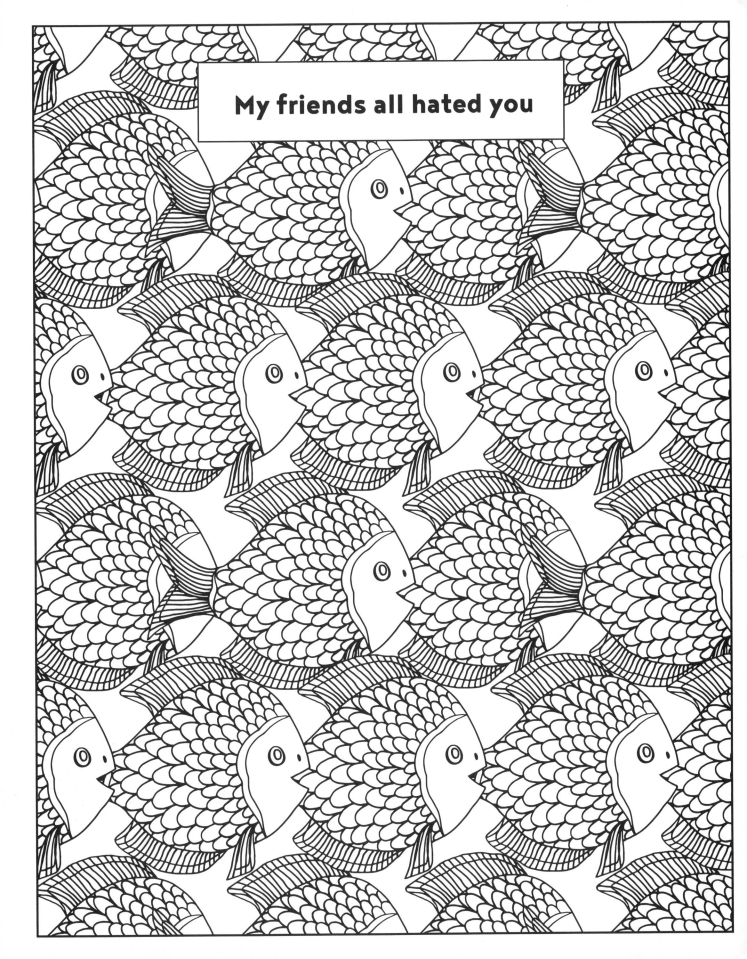

My friends all hated you

YOU'RE AN ASS HAT

Wait.

Come back.

You forgot your bullshit.

HATE is
a STRONG
word.
That's why
I USED IT.

Keep talking. I always yawn when I'm interested.

It's not me, it's you.

Everyone
deserves
to be happy.
Except you.
You're a prick.

EVERY DAY
WITHOUT YOU
IS A GIFT

You deserve someone worse

If only I could
unfuck you

I'm jealous of all the people who haven't met you

I could agree with you. But then we'd both be wrong.

It's mind
over matter.
I don't mind,
because you
really don't
matter.

I can explain it for you, but I can't understand it for you.

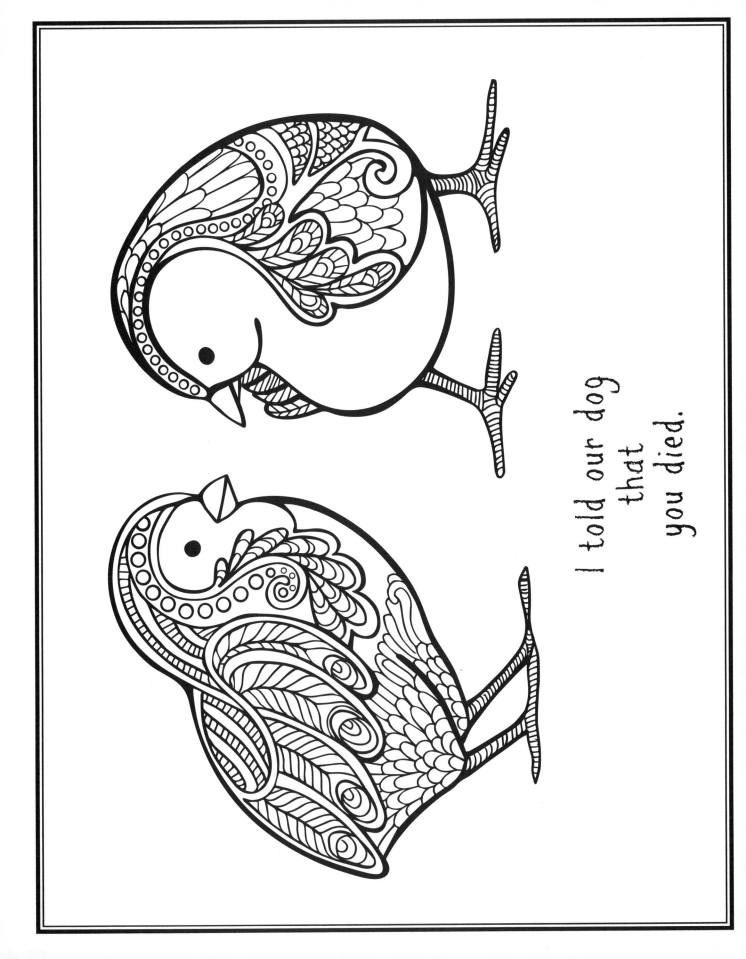

I told our dog
that
you died.

I hate your face

There's someone for everyone except you.

I hear what you're saying.   I just don't care.

Have a
nice life,
Asshole